W9-AYY-656

PRESENTED BY

Grant Williams
Class of 2009

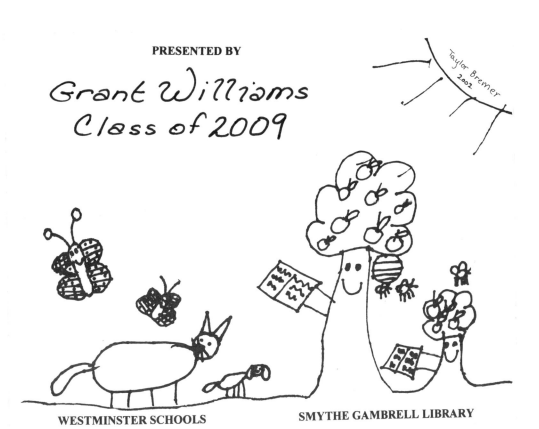

Taylor Bremer
2002

WESTMINSTER SCHOOLS          SMYTHE GAMBRELL LIBRARY

# THE CASTLE

# LIFE IN THE MIDDLE AGES

# THE CASTLE

by Kathryn Hinds

**BENCHMARK BOOKS**

MARSHALL CAVENDISH
NEW YORK

# TO MARIA

With special thanks to Alexandra Service,
Ph.D., Medieval Studies, University of York, England,
for her assistance in reading the manuscript

Translations on pp. 38–39 (from *The Canterbury Tales*, Geoffrey Chaucer) and 67 ("Non es meravelha s'eu chan," Bernart de Ventadorn; "A chantar m'er," Comtessa de Dia) are by Kathryn Hinds. The recipe on pp. 62–63 is adapted from *Fabulous Feasts: Medieval Cookery and Ceremony*, by Madeleine Pelner Cosman. The game on p. 52 is adapted from *Medieval Holidays and Festivals: A Calendar of Celebrations*, by Madeleine Pelner Cosman. The statement of homage on pp. 14–15 is quoted from Oliver I. Thatcher and Edgar H. McNeal, editors, *A Source Book for Medieval History*, New York, 1905, pp. 364–365.

Benchmark Books
Marshall Cavendish Corporation
99 White Plains Road, Tarrytown, New York 10591

Library of Congress Cataloging-in-Publication Data
Hinds, Kathryn, (date)
Life in the Middle Ages: The Castle / by Kathryn Hinds
p.    cm.
Includes bibliographical references and index.
Summary: Describes daily life in the castles of Europe from the years A.D. 500 to 1500.
ISBN 0-7614-1007-4 (lib. bdg.)
1. Castles—Juvenile literature. 2. Civilization, Medieval—Juvenile literature. [1. Castles.
2. Civilization, Medieval.] I. Title.
GT3550 .H56  2000  940.1—dc21  99-086102

Picture research by Rose Corbett Gordon, Mystic CT
*Art Resource, NY*: 13, 33, 40, 51- Giraudon; 22, 23- Erich Lessing; 48- The New York Public Library; 64-
The Pierpont Morgan Library. *Bibliotheca Philosophica Hermetica, Amsterdam*: 1.*Bridgeman Art
Library*: cover- Livre de las Chasse, c.1387, by Gaston Phebus, Bibliothèque Nationale Paris; 10- Crusades
of Godefroy de Bouillon, Chronique de Guillaume de Tyr, 14th c, Bibliothèque Nationale Paris; 15-
Knighting of Lancelot, La Quite de Saint Graal, 14th c, Bibliothèque Nationale Paris; 21- The Legend of
Tristan, 15th c, Musée Condé, Chantilly/INDEX; 30- From 19 books written for Edward IV by Jean du
Ries, Des Proprietez des Choses, 1482, British Library; 35- Chronicles of Enguerrand de Monstrelet,
Bibliothèque Nationale Paris; 37- Illustration by the Master of Cardinal of Bourbon from A History of the
Siege of Rhodes, 1483, by Guillaume Caoursin, Bibliothèque Nationale Paris; 38, 39- The Canterbury Tales
Ellesmere Manuscript, Private Collection; 54- Men and boys hawking, late 14th c, British Library;58-
Sienese Wedding Feast, c.1400, by Italian School, Private Collection; 66- Tapestry from Arras, 1420,
Musée des Arts Decoratifs, Paris; 70- From Vol. IV Froissart's Chronicles, late 15th c, British Library; 72-
A siege tower, Chronicle of France or of St. Denis, 14th c, Roy 16G VI f.74, British Library.*By permission of
the British Library, Ms. Royal 6: 8. Cliché Bibliothèque Nationale de France Paris*: 60. *The Image Works*: 18- Lee
Snider; 47- Mark Antman. *The Metropolitan Museum of Art*: 26. *North Wind Pictures*: 2, 17, 43.

Printed in Hong Kong
3   5   6   4   2

On the cover: Lords and ladies at the start of a hunt outside Paris,
by Gaston Phebus de Foix, around 1400
On the title page: Dinner at the house of a nobleman in the High Middle Ages

# CONTENTS

# ABOUT THE MIDDLE AGES

When we talk about the Middle Ages, we are talking about the period of European history from roughly 500 to 1500. Toward the end of this time, Italian writers and scholars known as humanists began to take a new interest in the literature and ideas of ancient Greece and Rome. The humanists wanted to create a renaissance, or rebirth, of ancient learning. They believed they were living in a new age, with a culture that was far superior to the culture of the previous ten centuries. So they called the years between the fall of Rome and their own time the Middle Ages, and the name has stuck.

The Italian humanists thought that the Middle Ages were dark, barbaric, ignorant, and without any kind of human progress. Today we often think of medieval times as a kind of storybook never-never land, with bold knights riding out on quests, jesters and wandering minstrels entertaining at sumptuous banquets, and kings and queens ruling from towered castles. But the real story about the Middle Ages is more fascinating than any fairy tale.

Just like life today, life in medieval times was full of complexity and variety. Although most people were peasants who spent their lives farming in the countryside, cities were growing and becoming increasingly important. Many women and men devoted themselves to religion, spending their lives in convents or monasteries. And of course there were castles, homes to kings, queens, nobles, and knights—and to large numbers of servants and craftspeople as well.

Medieval people had many of the same joys and sorrows, hopes and fears that we do, but their world was very different from ours. Forget about telephones, newspapers, computers, cars, and televisions. Step back into time, to the years 1100–1400, the High Middle Ages. And let history come alive. . . .

*An Italian knight of the High Middle Ages*

# 1
# LOYALTY AND PROTECTION

For hundreds of years, much of Europe was part of the Roman Empire. The rest of the continent was controlled by various tribal peoples, whom the Romans referred to as barbarians. When Rome fell to barbarian invaders in the fifth century, Europe was left with no central government, administration, or defense. Power was held by those who controlled the most land and who commanded the strongest forces of warriors. Europe's great landowners held sway over many small realms and were frequently at war with one another.

The lack of unity paved the way for invasions. During the eighth century Muslim warriors attacked from the east and south. They took over most of what is now Spain, much of which remained in Muslim hands for hundreds of years.

The conquerors were prevented from reaching farther into Europe by the Franks, a powerful tribe (from whom France takes its name). The Franks had recently developed a new style of warfare, which depended on troops of heavily armed warriors on horse-back—knights. This knightly warfare led to other developments: To get and hold power, a ruler needed the services and loyalty of

*French knights riding to battle during the fourteenth century. In their right hands they hold their lances, banners flying. On their chests they carry their shields. Each shield bears the knight's coat of arms, a design that belonged to him alone and was a way for other knights to identify him on the battlefield.*

many knights. In return for their loyalty, the ruler rewarded them with land and privileges. Men with the wealth to afford horses and equipment therefore rose in importance and power themselves, often becoming great nobles.

The greatest of the Frankish kings, Charlemagne (SHAR-luh-mane), took full advantage of these developments and united most of western Europe into a single empire. With the knights he commanded and the fortresses he built, Charlemagne was able to defend his empire well. It survived many attacks by the Muslims and also by the Vikings, who had begun to make frequent raids on western Europe's towns and villages. When Charlemagne died in 814, his empire quickly fell apart. But the kings who came after him followed his example in relying on knightly warfare. Many customs grew up around this style of warfare, giving shape to the system now known as feudalism.

# LORDS AND VASSALS

Feudalism was a military and political arrangement among kings and noblemen. By the High Middle Ages it had spread throughout much of western Europe and was particularly strong in France, England, and Germany. Its details varied from place to place, and in some areas, such as Scandinavia, it did not take hold at all. Wherever feudalism existed, however, its outline was basically the same.

In theory, a king owned all of the land in his kingdom. He kept a large portion of the land for his own use, and a great deal of land was also held by the Church. The king granted the use of the rest of the land to his vassals, the nobles who were his most powerful supporters. In return for these land grants, called fiefs, the vassals owed the king military service. They acknowledged the king as their lord, pledging to fight for him in person and also to provide a certain number of knights in time of war.

The king's vassals granted portions of their lands to lower-ranking nobles who, in return, promised knightly service. And just as the king's vassals had vassals of their own, these men, too, might take on vassals.

In addition to military service, vassals of all ranks had various other duties to their lords. These included escorting the lord on his travels, guarding his castle, and always being ready to welcome a visit from him. The lord had the right to summon his vassals to a council at any time. Vassals were usually expected to make money payments to the lord on certain occasions: when the lord granted them fiefs, when the lord's oldest daughter got married, and when his oldest son became a knight. If the lord was taken prisoner by an enemy, his vassals were required to pay ransom money to free him.

Beginning in the twelfth century, vassals who paid a tax called scutage did not have to perform military service for the lord. He used the tax money to hire mercenary soldiers instead. (Lords often preferred this—a vassal was only required to fight for the lord for forty days a year, but a hired soldier would serve the lord for as long as he was paid.)

The feudal bond was cemented by a ceremony in which the lord swore to protect and defend the vassal, and the vassal swore lifelong loyalty to the lord. This loyalty was not always upheld, however—royal vassals in particular rose in rebellion against their king quite often throughout the High Middle Ages.

*The king and queen of France, Jean le Bon ("the Good") and Jeanne de Boulogne, ride into Paris. They are accompanied by their many servants, vassals, and other retainers. Jean le Bon ruled from 1350 to 1364.*

# THE CEREMONY OF HOMAGE: A VASSAL'S VOWS

*The great hall of the lord's castle is crowded with knights, ladies, and members of the lord's household. There is an expectant silence in the room as all eyes are turned on the lord and his new vassal. With a great sense of importance and seriousness, lord and vassal face each other. The vassal kneels before the lord, and the lord takes the vassal's clasped hands between his own. In this position, the vassal swears to aid the lord, and the lord formally grants fiefs (lands) to the vassal and swears to aid him in turn. The oaths are sealed with a ceremonial kiss.*

This was homage, the ceremony that cemented the relationship between lord and vassal. Whenever a vassal took possession of land, he was required to do homage—or honor—to the lord. When a lord acquired new lands, he expected to receive homage from all the vassals on those lands.

Feudal relationships could be very complicated. A vassal might hold lands from more than one overlord. Sometimes the king of one country was even the vassal of the king of another country. England's Henry II, for example, had large landholdings in France, for which he was a vassal to the French king. The following thirteenth-century statement of homage reflects this kind of complexity:

> I, John of Toul, make known that I am the liege man of the lady Beatrice, countess of Troyes, and of her son, Theobald, count of Champagne, against every creature, living or dead, saving my allegiance to lord Enjorand of Coucy, lord

John of Arcis, and the count of Grandpré. If it should happen that the count of Grandpré should be at war with the countess and count of Champagne on his own quarrel, I will aid the count of Grandpré in my own person, and will sent to the count and the countess of Champagne the knights whose service I owe to them for the fief which I hold of them. But if the count of Grandpré shall make war on the countess and the count of Champagne on behalf of his friends and not in his own quarrel, I will aid in my own person the countess and count of Champagne, and will send one knight to the count of Grandpré for the service which I owe him for the fief which I hold of him, but I will not go myself into the territory of the count of Grandpré to make war on him.

# 2

# FEUDAL FORTRESSES

The greatest symbol of feudal life was the castle. In the 800s castles were being built all over what are now France, the Netherlands, Germany, and Italy. When William the Conqueror invaded England in 1066, he took with him an enthusiasm for castle building. In 1066 there were only half a dozen castles in England; by 1100 there were more than five hundred.

The castle was a protection against attackers and a center of power. Kings and lords used their castles to defend as well as to extend their territory. For example, after William the Conqueror's invasion of England, he faced many rebellions. Upon ending each one, he promptly ordered a castle to be built on the site of the rebellion. After that, the local people were firmly under his control. This tactic was valuable to many later kings and conquerors, too. In the thirteenth century King Edward I ringed Wales with some of the mightiest castles in Europe, using the strength of these fortresses to bring the Welsh under English rule.

## STRONG DEFENSES

The earliest European castles were usually a type called motte-and-bailey. Castle builders made a huge, steep, earthen mound—the motte (MAHT)—surrounded by a deep ditch. Around the top of the mound they erected a timber palisade, or wall. Within the wall was a stronghold called a keep or donjon, typically a tall, wooden, rectangular tower. Below the motte there was a large area enclosed by its own ditch and palisade. This was the bailey. Usually the castle's commander and his family lived in the keep, and his soldiers, with their horses and supplies, were housed in buildings in the bailey. In an emergency, everyone could go to the motte and the keep for safety.

Around 1100 most European castles were still constructed of wood. But during the next hundred years nearly all castles were built or rebuilt in stone. At some motte-and-bailey castles the palisade atop the motte was replaced by a high stone wall. At other places the bailey received the new fortifications, with a rectangular stone keep being placed within a very thick stone curtain wall.

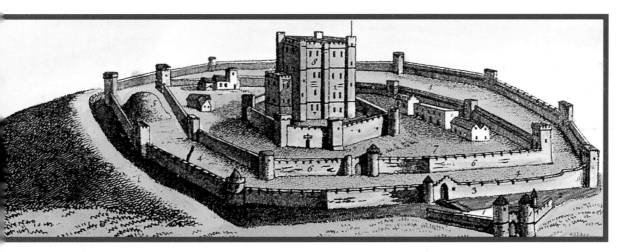

*A typical English castle of the eleventh or twelfth century, with 1) the gatehouse, 2) the ditch or moat, 3) the outer curtain wall, 4) the outer bailey, or courtyard, 5) an artificial mound, which may have served as an extra lookout point, 6) the inner curtain wall, 7) the inner bailey, and 8) the keep, which is built on top of a low motte, or mound.*

*A twelfth-century stone castle in Montbrun, France. The outer curtain wall is extremely high and is fortified by strong round towers. The square towers of earlier castles had a drawback: attackers could hide in their angles.*

The curtain was also used for completely new castles, and it gave Europe's feudal fortresses their distinctive "square-toothed" look. The top of the curtain was typically crenellated (KREH-nuh-lay-ted)—that is, it had alternating square or rectangular high and low sections. Each high section had an arrow loop, a narrow opening through which archers could shoot at attackers. At each low section, castle defenders could reach out to drop heavy stones, boiling liquids, and the like upon their enemies. The archers and other defenders stood on stone walkways built along the wall.

The curtain also had several towers, usually at the corners and at various points along the wall's length. At first the towers were rectangular, but later castle builders preferred round towers, which were easier to defend. From the towers the castle's soldiers could keep an eye on every part of the wall.

Since troops of warriors, as well as individuals, needed to be able to enter and leave the castle, there had to be one or two large doorways in the wall. These were vulnerable points, so they were heavily fortified with strong gatehouses. A gatehouse was made up of two massive towers, one on each side of the doorway, and a number of barriers. The first barrier was often a drawbridge over a ditch. (The ditch later came to be called the moat.) The drawbridge was raised in times of danger. Then there was a kind of gate called a portcullis. Beyond this was a set of heavy oak doors reinforced with iron bands. A stout wooden bar across the entryway made a final barrier. Some castles had two portcullises, two sets of doors, and two bars for an even stronger defense. By the thirteenth century, when castle building was at a peak, many castles were also given two curtain walls, one surrounding the other.

## INSIDE THE WALLS

At the simplest castles, a keep was the major building, with a storage area on the ground floor, a great hall above it, and living quarters on the top floor. Later, more elaborate castles had a number of buildings behind their curtain walls. The largest structure was the great hall, where the lord held court.

Early on, all the residents of the castle slept in the great hall.

# CASTLE COMFORTS

If you were to tour the ruins of a medieval castle, you would probably find it difficult to imagine anyone living in such a bare stone building. But these castles looked very different during the Middle Ages. Their outside walls were often whitewashed, so that they almost gleamed in the sunlight. Inside walls might be whitewashed as well. In the great hall and the nobles' chambers, the walls were frequently paneled with wood, painted (white, or in colors such as green and gold), and even embellished with murals. Hangings of painted cloth provided more decoration and helped cut down on drafts. In the fourteenth century tapestries, elaborately woven pictures, became popular wall coverings in castles all over Europe. Floors during this period, however, were generally bare wood or stone, strewn with sweet-smelling rushes and herbs.

The upper floors of castle buildings sometimes boasted large windows with glass panes. Often there was a cushioned window seat, where a lord or lady might sit comfortably—to enjoy a view of the castle garden, or to take advantage of the natural light in order to read, do needlework, and the like. Other lighting was supplied by candles (made from animal fat or, more expensively, beeswax) and oil lamps. A twelfth-century invention, the fireplace, provided both light and heat. Set into the wall so that the surrounding stones radiated heat, the fireplace was a great improvement over the central hearths of the past.

High, curtained beds, with feather-stuffed mattresses, quilts, and fur blankets, helped medieval lords and ladies stay warm while they slept. The bed was so large that usually there was little other furniture in the chamber—just a few stools and carved wooden chests for storage. Close to the chamber would be a garderobe (GAHR-drobe), a kind of indoor outhouse with a seat located over a chute that generally led to the moat. This was convenient, and more pleasant than using a chamber pot, but there was no toilet paper; hay was used instead.

Each floor of a castle typically had a place where water could be drawn from the well. Sometimes at the entrance to the great hall there was a stone basin for washing hands. A few castles had running water and a permanent bathhouse. But in most castles, when the lord or lady wanted to bathe, a wooden tub was set up in the chamber and filled with water heated in the fireplace. In good weather the tub might be placed in the garden and warmed by the sun. When great nobles traveled, they took along their bathtubs—and their beds and most of their other furniture—so that wherever they were, they could enjoy all the comforts of home.

*A lady greets visitors in her solar, or sitting room. This painting from a French manuscript of the 1400s shows a luxurious room with a tiled floor, beautifully decorated walls, and a glass window with shutters.*

*A sixteenth-century bed in a German castle. This is a bit more elaborate than the beds used by nobles of the High Middle Ages. Their beds were just as high off the ground, however, and they were usually enclosed by curtains made of heavy and expensive cloth.*

The lord and lady had some privacy behind a curtain or partition at one end. Later the lord and lady's chamber was often a room above the hall or on an upper floor of one of the castle towers. Sometimes the lord and lady had separate chambers. In the largest castles they might also have one or more sitting rooms, called solars.

The castle's residents ate their meals together in the great hall, so a kitchen building was usually close by. Food was stored in or near the hall and on the ground floors of towers. A well and several cisterns, which caught rainwater, supplied water to the castle. For fresh vegetables, herbs, and fruit, a kitchen garden and small orchard were sometimes located within the curtain wall.

All European castles had chapels. Sometimes a castle chapel was a small room tucked into a tower; sometimes it was as big as a regular church. Later castles often had more than one chapel—a private one for the lord and his family and a larger one for the other residents. Services were generally held in the chapel every day, and many lords required everyone in their household to attend these services at least once a week.

Since the castle's function was mainly military, within the walls there were usually barracks for soldiers. (At some castles, though, soldiers slept in the great hall or near their guardposts.) A

*A castle kitchen of the High Middle Ages looked much like this reconstruction in Kreuzenstein Castle in Austria.*

stable was located near the barracks. In addition to the knights' warhorses, the stable also housed saddle horses and packhorses. A blacksmith worked at a forge near the stable, making horseshoes and other necessities.

Horses were not the only animals within the castle walls. Cats ran about freely, protecting stored food from mice and rats. Hunting hounds had their kennels, and a lord's favorite dogs might follow him wherever he went in the castle. Many ladies had pet lapdogs. Falconry (hunting with the help of birds of prey) was a favorite sport with nobles all over Europe, so a mews where hawks and falcons were kept was also a common feature of castles.

Although the castle was a self-contained community in many ways, few castles stood in isolation for long. Many were built to command important towns in the first place. Others were not far from country villages. Numerous castles overlooked major waterways, river crossings, roads, or mountain passes. Wherever the castle stood, it often attracted farmers, merchants, and craftspeople into its shadow, offering them protection and a market for their goods. In this way many towns and cities—for example, Edinburgh, Scotland—grew up around castles.

# 3

# THE CASTLE COMMUNITY

A king or great noble held many castles, and during the course of a year he might visit several of them. In the twelfth and thirteenth centuries it was common for a lord to move on to a different location every month, or even every two weeks. Each castle generally had a "skeleton crew" of soldiers and servants who remained there all the time. Most of the household, however, traveled with the lord from place to place. A household of eight to thirty-five servants was typical at this time. These servants filled a variety of roles, but the most important task was to protect the lord, his family, and his valuables.

The group of knights and other military personnel who attended a lord were called his mesnie (may-NEE). Many members of the mesnie were permanent parts of the lord's household, although in England only the king had a regular bodyguard. Some of the mesnie were vassals on temporary military duty. Others were errants (AIR-unts), landless knights who often took service with a lord until they were able to become established landowners themselves. Many of a lord's knights served in nonmilitary positions when they were not needed to fight.

During the fourteenth century nobles became more settled, moving around much less than earlier. When they did travel, they took with them a small "riding household." This was separate from the main household, which was growing quite large. Most nobles now employed between thirty and seventy servants. The greatest lords, however, might have hundreds.

# GUESTS OF THE CASTLE

In addition to the lord, his family, and his household, a castle frequently housed guests—the lord's vassals, his allies, his over-lord or messengers from his overlord, relatives, and traveling churchmen among them. The lord and lady often raised and educated children from other noble families. After a battle or tournament, castle residents could also include nobles and knights being held for ransom. In the wake of war a lord often took hostages, usually family members of his enemy. He might hold these hostages in his castles for months or even years, as a guarantee that the hostages' families would keep peace with him, or because they had not paid the ransom. Such noble prisoners were usually kept under close guard but were well treated.

 *A castle's lord and lady and their son are accompanied on an outing by ladies-in-waiting and other servants. This scene is from a famous series of tapestries known as the Unicorn Tapestries. They were woven around the year 1500 in what is now Belgium.*

# SERVANTS WHO SPECIALIZED

The highest-ranking servant was the steward, or seneschal (SEN-uh-shul). His duty was to generally oversee the household and keep everything running smoothly. He was empowered to make many decisions on behalf of the lord. He also supervised the lord's manors, the farmland that produced most of the lord's wealth. (By the 1200s the lord often hired a second steward, usually a knight, for this duty.) In addition, the steward might be the household's treasurer, although large establishments usually required a separate treasurer to keep track of expenses.

Another extremely important servant was the cook, who was highly paid for his specialized skills. He often supervised a very large staff. Some households also employed a kitchen clerk to handle and record food expenses. But it was the cook, or sometimes the steward, who made the decisions about what food to buy and prepare.

Large households needed a servant to keep order in the great hall, where everyone in the castle ate together. In the king of England's household this well-paid servant was the hall marshal; in the halls of great nobles a chief gentleman-usher often filled this job. His tasks included making sure that diners were seated according to their rank, overseeing the waiters, and, when necessary, breaking up fistfights during the meal.

The stable marshal was in charge of everything to do with the stableyard. He supervised huntsmen and the servants who cared for the lord's horses, hounds, and falcons. He also made sure that carts were in good repair, that saddles and other gear were well taken care of, and that the castle was always supplied with plenty of feed for the horses.

Every noble household employed at least one chaplain, a priest who was in charge of the castle's chapel and worship services. The chaplain oversaw the rest of the chapel staff, which could include other priests, caretakers for the chapel's valuable items, and perhaps a few singers. Occasionally chaplains also fulfilled the roles of steward and treasurer. Since chaplains and most other priests in noble households were well educated, they could act as secretaries and accountants as well.

Another specialized servant was the wardrober, who took care of the lord's costly clothes, jewels, and the like. Because he handled so many valuables and was well trusted, he might also act as the lord's treasurer. An almoner was a servant with different financial responsibilities: he distributed the lord's charitable donations to the poor.

Most lords kept a barber on hand—during the Middle Ages barbers not only cut hair and gave shaves but also performed dentistry and minor surgery. Some noble households included a physician or apothecary (a person who made medicines); others called in these medical specialists only when needed.

# JACKS (AND JILLS) OF ALL TRADES

Many servants had general functions: the same man might wait at table, deliver messages, make purchases at local markets, and take care of other matters as needed. Some servants were craftspeople part of the time, making candles, soap, and the like.

The lord's most trusted servants tended to be his personal attendants. These were frequently lower-ranking noblemen, and they might do anything from helping the lord dress to going on diplomatic missions for him. In fact, a number of the chief servants

*Servants dye cloth in a castle workshop.*

in a castle could be of noble birth. In France and Italy, many of the lord's attendants and upper servants were his own cousins and other relatives.

Even many non-nobles were ranked as gentlemen, the servants who did the least physical labor. Lower in status were the valets. They often performed skilled jobs and had a great deal of responsibility. Valets' duties could include anything from assisting the stable marshal to making the lord's bed to slaughtering livestock. The lowest-ranking servants, grooms, had the hardest and dirtiest tasks, such as scrubbing pots and cleaning out stables. Valets and grooms typically came from peasant families in the villages near the castle.

In the Middle Ages, nearly all servants were male, and most of them were unmarried. If a servant was married, his wife and children usually did not live at the castle with him. An upper servant's wife, however, might become an attendant or lady-in-waiting to the lord's wife.

Occasionally a steward's or clerk's widow might take over his job. Otherwise, the only female servants in a castle were laundresses, caregivers for the lord's children, and the lady's personal attendants. Except for those who did the humblest jobs of the lady's chamber, these attendants, like the lord's, tended to be from noble families. Most were girls and young unmarried women. In addition, some of the lady's attendants were young boys, who ran light errands for her. Boys also worked in the kitchen and the bakery and did such chores as dusting.

For the most part, castle servants seem to have been contented with their lot. It was not unusual for a servant to be employed in the same household for twenty years or more, sometimes rising from groom to valet and even to gentleman. Nobles' servants enjoyed a fairly high standard of living, for in addition to their salaries, they received tips, rewards, and holiday bonuses. The lord also gave them free clothing, food, and shelter. The highest-ranking servants might even have their own rooms, and a number of servants had servants of their own.

# 4

# A LORD'S DUTIES

A great lord's life centered around land. His manors supplied his household with wool, eggs, milk, grain, meat, and other farm products to use or sell. The people living on his land paid him rents and various taxes, tolls, fines, and fees. Land was wealth, and landownership made the lord powerful. The more land a lord held, the more vassals and other followers he could command. There were French lords—the dukes of Normandy and Aquitaine, the counts of Anjou and Champagne—whose holdings were so large that they rivaled kings.

Although lords received their fiefs from the king, they felt very strongly that the land they held belonged to them. Custom supported this, and usually when a lord died, his holdings passed to one or more of his sons. If he had no sons, in most areas a daughter could inherit. Whatever the arrangement, the important thing was to keep the land in the family.

Lords were willing to go to great lengths to keep and increase the lands they held. They sought favor with their overlord in the hope that he would grant them additional fiefs. They made marriages and alliances that brought new territory into their hands. Sometimes they used the legal system to prove that they

*Planting the fields surrounding a French castle, from a manuscript of the early 1400s. One of the gentlemen strolling outside the castle wall may be the lord himself.*

were the rightful owners of lands held by someone else. All too often, they turned to force.

# FIGHTING FOR LORD AND LAND

Warfare was a fact of life, even a way of life, for knights and nobles. Part of a noble's obligation to his overlord was to fight for him. War could arise at any time, but in much of medieval Europe there was a traditional season for battles. This fighting season began after the Feast of Saint John (June 24) and continued for forty days, the amount of time that vassals were required to bear arms for their lords. Conflicts often lasted longer, of course, but generally no fighting was done in the winter.

Not only did lords fight each other, but a single lord's vassals frequently fought among themselves. Then the lord might feel the need to step in to stop this bloody quarreling in his territories. For example, in the 1170s the lords of southern France were violent rivals for control of the region. Count Richard of Poitou (who later became England's King Richard the Lion-Hearted) went to war to put an end to their feuding and to bring the territories firmly under his control. His actions were so brutal that the quarrelsome lords of southern France at last united—to resist Richard.

In fact, vassals often rebelled against their lords, in spite of their vows of loyalty. Nobles were very protective and proud of their rights. If they felt that their lord was limiting their power too much or making too many demands on them, they were usually

*A fourteenth-century battle between the French and English in the Hundred Years' War. To the left sits the king of France, surrounded by the commanders of his army.*

quick to rise against him. When a vassal saw the opportunity to gain more land and power, it was easy for him to find reasons for rebellion.

# WARRIORS FOR GOD

Another kind of medieval warfare occurred for very different reasons. The Christian faith had a powerful effect on medieval European society. The Church taught that all people were basically sinful, but that acts of penance could earn forgiveness for sin. One of the most powerful acts of penance was going on a pilgrimage, and the greatest pilgrimage was to Jerusalem, the scene of several important events in the life of Jesus.

Christian Europe also had a long-standing rivalry with the Muslim world. In 1095 the pope, head of the Christian church in western Europe, sent out a call for knights to go to Jerusalem to take the holy city from its Muslim rulers. This was the beginning of the First Crusade, a pilgrimage and at the same time a war fought for God.

The crusaders faced great difficulties and danger—it was a long, hard journey just to get to the Middle East. They knew they would be away from home for between one and three years, and they worried about how their families and lands would fare in their absence. Crusading was also extremely expensive, costing a knight up to three times his usual annual income. Nevertheless, numerous lords joined the First Crusade with great enthusiasm. The idea of winning forgiveness from sin (and a place in Heaven) by going to war—the thing they had been trained to do since childhood—was very powerful. Crusading quickly became one of the things expected of the perfect knight.

The Crusades continued to occur on and off throughout the twelfth and thirteenth centuries. Many knights never returned to

*Knights Hospitallers defend their kingdom against a Muslim army.*

Europe—in addition to those who were killed in battle, great numbers died of thirst, starvation, or disease. Some lords and their followers settled in the Holy Land, for the crusaders established several realms of their own, the most important being the Kingdom of Jerusalem. Other men stayed to become Knights Templar or Knights Hospitaller, members of religious military groups sworn to defend the Holy Land and assist pilgrims there. The Templars and the Hospitallers built some of the Middle Ages' greatest castles. Many of these can still be seen in the Middle East today.

# CHAUCER'S KNIGHT

Geoffrey Chaucer, who lived from about 1340 to 1400, was one of the greatest writers in English literature. His most famous book is *The Canterbury Tales*, in which a group of people on a pilgrimage to the shrine of Saint Thomas à Becket, in Canterbury, entertain one another by telling stories. One of the pilgrims is a knight, accompanied by his son, a squire. Chaucer's knight has taken part in a number of crusades, including wars against the Muslims of Spain and non-Christian peoples of eastern Europe (these wars were also thought of as crusades). Crusading had become part of the knightly ideal, and Chaucer wanted his character to be a model of knighthood. The squire, on the other hand, has had no real battle experience yet but is a fashionable master of courtly skills. Here, in a modern English adaptation, is Chaucer's description of the knight and his son:

*A knight there was—and that a worthy man—*
*That from the time that he first began*
*To ride to battle, he loved chivalry,*
*Truth and honor, freedom and courtesy.*
*Full worthy was he in his lord's war,*
*And thereto had he ridden, no man so far,*
*In both Christendom and in heathen places.*
*He was ever honored for his worthiness.*
*When Alexandria was won, he was there.*
*At table he had the place of honor*
*Full often for his deeds in Prussia.*

*The Squire*

*In Lithuania had he fought, and in Russia—*
*More than any man of his degree.*
*In Grenada also at the siege was he. . . .*
*. . .*
*His fame was the kind most highly prized,*
*And brave as he was, he was also wise.*
*Like a maiden, his bearing was meek,*
*And no rudeness did he ever speak*
*To anyone in any rank of life.*
*He was a true, perfect, noble knight.*
*. . .*
*With him there was his son, a young squire,*
*A lover and a lively bachelor*
*With curling hair about his shoulders.*
*He was twenty years old, I guess, no older.*
*Of his stature he was of average length,*
*And wonderfully agile, with great strength.*
*. . .*
*He was singing or whistling all the day—*
*He was as fresh as is the month of May.*
*Short was his gown, with sleeves long and wide.*
*Well could he sit on horse and beautifully ride.*
*He could make tunes, with words to fit them right,*
*Joust, and also dance, and well draw and write.*

**The Knight**

# PEACEFUL PASTIMES

When a lord was not at war, there was still plenty for him to do. He had his lands to look after, and he had his various peacetime duties to his overlord. In addition he usually had responsibilities in the justice system.

In England the most serious crimes were tried only by the king's court, while in France and Germany they were tried by kings and also by great lords. These crimes included treason, making false money, theft, kidnapping, arson, and murder and other violent

*A nobleman and his friends take a break from their hunting to have a grand meal outdoors.*

offenses. Accused criminals were sometimes briefly held in a castle tower or storage area while they awaited trial, but criminals were rarely sentenced, as we might think, to be thrown into dungeons. During most of the Middle Ages, people convicted in the high courts were usually either executed or maimed. For example, a thief might be punished by having his hand cut off.

Each lord administered his own court to handle the less serious and nonviolent crimes that occurred on his lands. Usually the lord's steward presided over the court for him. Convicted criminals were charged fines, which were paid to the lord. In fact, such fines often made up a good portion of a lord's income.

Another source of income and prestige for a lord was to hold a post in the king's government. (Kings paid handsome salaries to their officials and often gave them additional rewards.) English nobles sometimes went to great lengths to get themselves or their friends appointed as sheriffs, the officers in charge of individual shires, or counties. Chancellor, chamberlain, treasurer, and constable were some of the other royal posts a lord could fill in England. Knights and lesser lords in France held office as viscounts (similar to English sheriffs), seneschals, and overseers of trade fairs, among other things.

When a lord had some free time, a favorite activity was hunting. Most lords set aside large portions of their land as game preserves. Knights and nobles rode on horseback when they hunted, using dogs and falcons to help them bring down game. Hunting was good exercise, and it supplied the household with fresh meat. Since it required excellent riding skills, it also helped keep knights in shape for battle.

# 5

# A LADY'S DAYS

In theory, only men took part in the feudal relationship between lord and vassal. Most medieval priests, lawmakers, and other thinkers believed that women were too weak, unintelligent, and prone to sin to be trusted in positions of power. Actually, though, it was common for noblewomen to hold fiefs—sometimes very large and important ones.

Not only could a daughter inherit land, but a widow kept from one-third to one-half of her dead husband's property. Since warfare and other dangerous activities played a major part in the lives of medieval men, their death rate was very high. One study has shown that between 1350 and 1500, 25 percent of English noblemen never reached the age of forty. The result was that many women were widowed and many men had no living sons to inherit their lands.

Like a male holder of a fief, an heiress or widow pledged loyalty and support to her overlord, and she generally fulfilled the same duties as a male vassal. However, she was not expected—or trained—to provide military service. If she married or remarried, this responsibility fell on her husband. For this reason, the overlord of a noble heiress or widow had a great deal of control over whom she married. If she refused to marry the man her lord picked for

*Three noblewomen sit at the head table during a feast. From a balcony above them, minstrels entertain with music. The women's elaborate headdresses were popular during the fifteenth century, especially in France.*

her, if she wished to marry someone of her own choice, or if she wanted to remain unmarried (though this was rare), she was required to pay the lord a large fee.

A woman who held a fief could have many vassals of her own. She presided over the justice system on her lands and performed other duties expected of a lord. Sometimes her husband took on authority over her territory, but it seems that in most places the heiress or widow was usually able to exercise her full rights to rule.

# ELEANOR OF AQUITAINE

One of medieval Europe's most notable and remarkable women was Eleanor of Aquitaine. In 1137, at the age of fifteen, she inherited her father's vast landholdings in southern France. A few months later she was married to the seventeen-year-old son of the king of France. Shortly after the marriage the king died, and Eleanor was crowned queen of France beside her husband, the new King Louis VII. For several years Eleanor had great influence over Louis, advising him on matters of statecraft and war.

In 1145 Louis announced that he would undertake a crusade to the Holy Land, where the crusader kingdoms established after the First Crusade were under threat. The Second Crusade departed France in the summer of 1147. Eleanor and many other noblewomen—some of them dressed and armed like men—were among the warrior-pilgrims. Indeed, Eleanor's great wealth and numerous vassals made the crusade possible.

The expedition was, however, a disaster. Many men were lost to hardships and ambushes on the way to the Holy Land. The crusaders won no new territory, and the existing crusader kingdoms were as insecure as ever. And during the course of the crusade, Eleanor determined to end her marriage to Louis. The king, however, would not hear of it. After celebrating Easter 1149 in Jerusalem, they finally returned to France.

Soon afterward, Eleanor gave birth to a daughter, their second. Since Eleanor had not given Louis a son and heir during fifteen years of marriage, he seems to have decided that divorcing her was now his best course. With the consent of the Church, the pair were separated in 1152. Louis kept their two daughters, but Eleanor kept her lands, to which she returned.

Two months later Eleanor married Henry, Duke of Normandy

and Count of Anjou. She had met him the year before, at court in Paris, when he was eighteen and a new-made knight. The joining of their lands made the pair a formidable force. In 1154 Henry, grandson of Henry I, became king of England. This began a long period of rivalry between the kings of England and France.

Eleanor and Henry had five sons and three daughters. Henry was a busy and restless king, frequently off to war or making the rounds of his French landholdings. When he was away, Eleanor ruled England in his place. By 1170, however, she had grown tired of England and of Henry's wandering ways. She returned to her ancestral lands, to the city of Poitiers. Here she established her own court, where she hosted the best poets and musicians in France. This was a splendid time, but it did not last long. In 1173 Henry's three oldest sons rebelled against him, and Eleanor supported their cause. After Henry quashed the rebellion, he took Eleanor back to England and confined her to one of his castles. She was not released until 1185. Four years later Henry died, and his son Richard (the Lion-Hearted) succeeded him as king.

Richard was Eleanor's favorite son, and she now returned to a place of honor and power. Once more Eleanor ruled as Queen of England, for Richard spent nearly all his reign in France or on crusade (and for two years after the Third Crusade, he was held prisoner in Germany by the Holy Roman Emperor). When Richard died in 1199, his brother John became king. Eleanor assisted this son, too, in establishing his rule. She went on diplomatic missions for him and was even besieged by his enemies in the French castle of Mirebeau. But after this Eleanor retired from public life. She returned to her beloved Poitiers, and there she died in 1204, at the age of eighty-two. She had lived a long and remarkable life.

# WIVES AND MOTHERS

A noblewoman who did not hold fiefs of her own still had a very important position. She assisted her husband in many ways, and she was generally in charge of the household. She oversaw all of the servants and might even supervise the management of the lord's manors. The lady often had responsibility for the family finances and for making payments to retainers, employees, charities, and so on. She greeted and entertained important guests for her husband, and sometimes she even fulfilled his official duties, such as holding court.

In the feudal point of view, however, the lady's most important function was to provide the lord with sons who could inherit his fiefs. Noblewomen often had ten or more children. But even among nobles, many mothers died in childbirth because medieval medical knowledge was very limited. Babies, too, frequently died during or soon after birth. Because of these dangers, during a lady's pregnancy the noble family's chaplain said special prayers for both her and her unborn child. The lord and lady themselves were likely to pray to various saints for a safe birth and might also make a pilgrimage to a saint's shrine.

Even if a lady lived through childbirth, her babies were cared for largely by servants. The medieval noblewoman did not breast-feed her child but, according to the custom of the time, hired a wet nurse to do this.* However, as her children grew older, the lady did

*This custom may have developed because people believed that if a nursing mother became pregnant, her milk would no longer be good for the baby she was breastfeeding. Noblewomen were expected to bear as many children as possible, and so their frequent pregnancies prevented them from being able to nurse their own babies, according to the beliefs of the time.

*Surrounded by relatives, a mother cradles her newborn in her arms.*

play a role in their education. She also took part in the training of other children in the household, usually children of her husband's vassals or allies.

Altogether, a lady's days were very full. In her leisure time she enjoyed many of the same activities as the lord, such as playing chess and hunting with falcons. She also did fine embroidery and weaving. A favorite pastime was reading. In fact, medieval noble-women tended to read a great deal more than their husbands did. Ladies read the Psalms and other religious works, but romances were especially popular. These medieval romances were long poems that often told stories of the knights and ladies of King Arthur's Court. The tales were full of love, magic, and heroic deeds. They are still enjoyed by many people today.

*A lady seated at an elaborate reading desk enjoys her book.*

# LADIES AT WAR

The lord of a castle was often away. In his absence the lady ruled his lands—and protected them if necessary. If the lord died, leaving his lands to his son, it often happened that the heir was still a child. Then, in most places, the boy's mother became his guardian until he was an adult. This too put the lady in the position of having to rule and protect the land.

There are a number of accounts of noble wives, mothers, widows, and heiresses defending castles. In 1341 while the countess of Brittany's husband was away, one of their castles came under attack. The countess was there and organized the defense. She assigned the castle's women and children to tear out the courtyard's paving stones and take them to the soldiers on the wall, who dropped the stones down on the attackers. The countess even led out an army to chase off the enemy. Although it was not common, throughout the Middle Ages there were other noblewomen who, when necessary, personally fought off invaders, led armies, recruited soldiers, and even ordered the building of castles.

The medieval lady did not always stay home at the castle. Often she went along with the lord on his travels. A number of noble-women even accompanied their husbands on the Crusades. There are some records of women fighting in battles in the Middle East, but it is hard to tell if any of them were ladies; many other women also went on the Crusades. Noblewomen traveled without their husbands, too, touring the family's different castles and manors, visiting the overlord's court, going on pilgrimage, and the like. These ladies were not the timid princesses of the average fairy tale!

# 6

# A NOBLE UPBRINGING

T he babies of nobles were always born at home, usually with the help of one or more midwives. Newborns were given very tender care. They were bathed in lukewarm water at least once a day; gently rubbed with oil; wrapped in soft, warm swaddling clothes; kept away from strong light; and picked up whenever they cried. Many noble infants had cradles in which they could be rocked. In some castles babies had their own room, opening off the mother's chamber, heated by a special stove so that they would not catch cold.

In normal circumstances, a baby was baptized, or brought into the Christian faith, when it was a week old. The child also received its name at this time. During the High Middle Ages noble babies were usually named after a relative, but sometimes they were named after a saint, or occasionally after a legendary hero.

A lord and lady's children were closely attended as they grew. When they began to walk, the wet nurse or parents made sure that there was a bench nearby to which they could hold on. Because toddlers fell down a lot, they were given padded bonnets to protect their heads. By the thirteenth century many noble children had

*A noble family of fifteenth-century France. The children wear miniature versions of adult clothing. They appear to be listening closely to their father's advice.*

walkers, little chairs with wheels on the legs. Medieval writers instructed parents and wet nurses to use gentleness, encouragement, and praise with toddlers as they learned to walk and talk.

Up till the age of three, both boys and girls were cared for by their mothers and wet nurses. Then a boy's nurse might be replaced by a tutor, and at the age of four he might start learning to ride horses. A girl's nurse often continued to care for her and serve her long after breastfeeding was done with. Until the children were about seven, their mother had the main responsibility for teaching them basic Christian beliefs, important prayers, and some of the Psalms.

# BLIND MAN'S BUFF

In medieval Europe, people of all ages and all social ranks enjoyed playing games together. One of the oldest and most popular games was blind man's buff. It is still fun to play today. To start, select one player to be It, and cover his or her eyes. Any piece of cloth can make a good blindfold, but to give a more medieval flavor to the game, use a hood or an animal mask. In any case, It should not be able to see anything at all.

The other players make a circle around It, and one of them gently turns It around a few times. Then the players, one at a time, run to the center of the circle and lightly "buffet," or tap, It. It tries to catch these players before they can return to their places. When a player is caught, It must identify him or her—without being able to see, of course! The first person whom It names correctly now becomes It, and the game starts all over again!

During this part of childhood there was also lots of time to play. Toys included rattles, whistles, drums, blocks, balls, tops, see-saws, miniature windmills, small wooden boats, clay animals, hobby horses, rocking horses, and marionettes. Noble girls might have several dolls, and boys had wooden swords and shields. Sometimes children got permission to play with things that belonged to their parents—their mother's jewelry, for example. Boys and girls played imaginatively, too, both on their own and in groups. They also enjoyed many games, in which adults often joined.

At about the age of seven, girls and boys were separated. Training for the roles they would play as adults now began in earnest.

# THE FUTURE KNIGHT

After age seven, the oldest son was generally educated at home under the supervision of his father, since he would one day inherit his father's position and property. By the age of nine, a younger son was usually sent to the castle of another noble—an uncle, a friend of his father's, or his father's overlord. There he became a page, serving his foster father's knights and learning from them. If a noble family had many sons, one or two of them might be sent to a monastery or, a little later, to a university. These sons would be educated for careers in the church, in law, or in government administration.

Most noble boys were destined to become knights. Until the twelfth century, it was unusual for them to learn how to read. Their education focused on archery, horsemanship, and other warrior skills.

Even recreation educated them for the future. Learning to play chess taught them to think strategically. Active games, including various ball games, helped them learn to react quickly, to think on their feet, and to handle themselves in the midst of action. Many of these games were played together by a large group of boys being trained at the castle, so the future knights also learned about teamwork.

Much of a page's training involved simply observing the life of his foster father's court, learning from the examples of the adults around him. The behavior of the knights and ladies was reinforced by songs and stories that taught the ideals of chivalry. A page learned that the perfect knight was brave, loyal, generous, and honorable. As a Christian warrior, he was expected to be just and truthful, modest and merciful. He should use his strength and skill to protect the Church and all those who were weaker than he. Beginning in the twelfth century, the ideal knight was also what we might call a perfect gentleman. He was courteous and well mannered, he respected all noblewomen, and he faithfully served his chosen lady. His speech was gracious. He should be able to sing, play at least one musical instrument, and dance. He might even learn to read and write—not only in his own language, but also in Latin, and perhaps in one or more foreign languages.

At about age twelve knightly training became intense. Swordsmanship, wrestling, attacking targets while on horseback, and hunting were skills that had to be mastered now. At the age of fifteen the page generally became a squire. He served one particular knight, caring for his horse and armor, waiting on him at table, and following him to war. Two to four years later, the squire was at last ready to become a knight himself.

 *Two boys learn the art of falconry, hunting with the help of trained hawks, or falcons.*

The young man could be knighted by his foster father, his own father, his father's overlord, or the knight who had trained him. Sometimes all the squires in a household were knighted together by the lord of the castle. The knighting could occur on a special occasion or before an upcoming battle. Some young men were knighted after a battle, right on the battlefield, in recognition of their achievements.

Initiation into knighthood was usually a splendid event. The ceremonies, as they took shape in the twelfth century, began with a bath to cleanse the body. Then the knight-to-be sat up through the night in the castle chapel, praying to purify his soul. In the morning he attended a religious service, followed by breakfast with friends and family. Then he dressed in a new set of garments, all white, and was led to the place of the knighting. His father and other knights helped him into his armor and presented him with a sword that had been blessed by a priest. The young man kissed the hilt of the sword. At last the man who was knighting him gave him the accolade, the kiss or blow on the cheek that officially made the squire a knight. (One medieval writer explained that the blow—which often knocked the young man to the ground—was supposed to help the new knight remember the importance of keeping his vows.) Once the ceremony was over, it was time for feasting and perhaps even a tournament, where the new knight could show off his prowess.

# FROM CHILD TO BRIDE

Like their knightly brothers, most noble girls were also carefully trained. They were usually taught at home by their mothers, often with the help of tutors or governesses. Some girls went to convents for their education (a number of these girls later became nuns), and some went to the court of another noble. Wherever a girl was educated, training in good manners, hospitality, and household management were of high importance. Many of these things were learned by observing the lady of the castle and following her example.

It was also very common for the daughters of lords to learn to read and, often, to write. Some mastered more than one language. Many studied arithmetic and became familiar with land laws in preparation for their future. Like their brothers, they were taught to ride, to train and hunt with falcons, and to play chess. The ideal lady also knew how to embroider and weave, sing and dance, play a musical instrument, and tell stories. Some basic medical knowledge along the lines of first aid—was also considered useful for the future wife of a knight.

As a noble girl was being educated, plans were already under way for her marriage. In the Middle Ages, nearly all marriages were arranged by the families of the bride and groom. Although the Church decreed that the couple had to consent to the marriage, in practice they often had no say in the matter. Young women and men of the peasantry had the most freedom of choice. Nobles had the least, since their marriages could have a huge impact on landholding and politics. Marriage was a way to make alliances and to gain additional lands. It had nothing to do with love—frequently the bride and groom did not even meet until the wedding.

According to the law, a girl had to be at least twelve to get married, and a boy had to be fourteen. Most noble families did stay well within these guidelines: It was common for men to be in their twenties when they married, and brides were usually between the ages of fourteen and eighteen. But among royalty and the very

*A noble Italian bride and groom of the early 1400s are congratulated by their families.*

highest nobles, couples were often engaged when they were babies or toddlers. Sometimes young children actually got married. For example, in 1160 the five-year-old heir of the king of England was married to the three-year-old daughter of the king of France.

Even though a noble marriage rarely started with love, love often grew. One lord, still grieving over his wife many years after her death, wrote about how he had composed songs and poems for her while she was alive. Most couples at least shared a bond of common purpose as they strove together to hold and rule their land and pass it on to the next generation.

# 7

# FESTIVITIES, TOURNAMENTS, AND TROUBADOURS

Weddings, knightings, baptisms—these were some of the most festive occasions in the medieval castle. Splendid celebrations occurred for holidays, too. The most important holidays were Christmas and Easter, which honored Christ's birth and his rising from the dead. Kings and great lords often held a Christmas court and an Easter court, their major gatherings of the year. Along with religious services, feasting, and entertainment, judgments were passed, high councils met, and lords and vassals renewed their pledges.

For Christmas in many places the castle was decorated with holly and ivy, and a huge Yule log burned in the great hall's fireplace. The lord presented gifts of new clothing to all in his household. Kings often gave their knights and retainers lavish presents, such as saddle horses, jewels, gold and silver cups, and costly garments. The Christmas festivities lasted a full twelve days, from December 25 to January 6. Songs, dances, games, and feasting were part of the celebration for young and old, noble and servant alike.

*Lords and ladies circle around in a stately dance. Dancing was an enjoyable part of many medieval feasts and celebrations.*

In February or March, forty-six days before Easter, the season of Lent began. During this serious time of prayer and penance, the cross in the castle chapel was covered with a shroud, a piece of cloth like the kind used to wrap a dead body. On the Friday preceding

Easter, the cross was buried or hidden in a special place in the chapel. The next night every candle and fire in the castle was put out. Then, with great ceremony, a new fire was kindled and a special Easter candle was lit. In the chapel the priests and others held an all-night vigil. When Easter morning dawned, they brought out the cross and placed it upon the altar. A solemn and joyful service was held, followed by a bountiful feast.

Advent (several weeks before Christmas) and Lent were seasons when people were expected to put aside many of their worldly concerns and focus their thoughts on religion. During these times, too, the Church declared the Truce of God, when no one should commit any kind of violence. In particular, lords were expected not to engage in warfare during the Truce of God. Many tried to keep the peace, but few were successful on a regular basis.

# KNIGHTLY CONTESTS

Shortly after Easter the season of tournaments began. These contests among knights, organized by great lords, were a sport, a form of entertainment, and practice for battle. When a tournament was proclaimed, hundreds of knights and their squires came from far and wide to attend. Spectators, too, flocked to the gathering. Tents were set up on open land, and the inns of the nearest town overflowed.

A festival atmosphere surrounded tournaments. They attracted horse dealers, armor makers, food sellers, and a variety of other merchants. Storytellers, minstrels, and acrobats were among the performers who found enthusiastic audiences. Ladies came dressed in their finest, ready to cheer on their favorite knights. There were stone-throwing contests, wrestling matches, and dice games. There

# FOOD FIT FOR A KING

Nobles and their households ate well. Unlike most peasants, castle residents were usually able to eat meat almost every day. Beef and mutton were the most commonly eaten red meats, but veal, lamb, and pork were also popular. Chicken was prepared in a variety of ways and was greatly enjoyed. Game animals frequently graced noble tables: deer, wild boar, and duck, as well as geese, pigeons, herons, and other birds.

During Advent and Lent, and on Wednesdays, Fridays, and Saturdays all year-round, devout medieval Christians did not eat meat. Fish (which was not considered meat by the Church) was consumed instead. Noble households enjoyed an enormous variety of seafood, but among the favorites were salmon, trout, herring, lobster, crab, and oysters.

On a holiday or other special occasion, meals became elaborate feasts with numerous courses. In addition to the more common meats, there were delicacies such as roast swan or peacock. Exotic imported fruits—oranges, lemons, dates, figs—were used as ingredients in special recipes. Rich sauces were seasoned with cinnamon, ginger, pepper, and other expensive spices from the East. Edible flowers decorated cakes and tarts. Sometimes the cook concocted spectacular food sculptures, often made of marzipan. You can make this delicious confection yourself.

To make marzipan, you will need:

1 pound blanched almonds
a little ice water
2 egg whites
1⅓ cup confectioner's sugar
¼ cup orange juice or lemon juice
Optional: a couple pinches of cinnamon, cloves, and/or ginger
For decoration: food coloring (medieval people used edible plants—parsley, violets, and saffron, for example—to get their food dyes, but you can buy yours at the supermarket)

Grind the almonds—the medieval way is to use a mortar and pestle, but you could use a blender or food processor. Every so often add a bit of ice water to the almonds so that they do not become too oily. You should end up with a thick paste.

Put the egg whites into a large bowl and beat them until they form peaks. Beat in the confectioner's sugar a little at a time.

Put the almond paste into the bowl, too, and add the spices if you want to. Wet your fingers with the juice and knead the mixture for ten minutes. Whenever it feels too sticky, add a bit more juice.

Now you have marzipan. Divide it into as many portions as you have colors. Wrap each portion separately (in waxed paper, aluminum foil, or plastic wrap) and put it into the refrigerator for a day or two.

When you are ready to work with the marzipan, let it warm to room temperature first. Take each portion one at a time. Squeeze a few drops of food coloring onto it, then knead it until the coloring is completely mixed in. (Wet your fingers with ice water if the marzipan is too sticky.) When you have colored all of the marzipan, you are ready to sculpt it into fruit or animal shapes or whatever you can imagine.

*From a safe distance, a queen and her ladies-in-waiting watch a furiously fought tournament.*

was dancing in the meadows and on town greens. Outside the tents and in the streets of the town, tables were set up for feasting by candlelight.

In the twelfth and thirteenth centuries, the actual tournament was a mock battle between two groups of knights on horseback. The groups assembled at opposite ends of a huge field. A signal was given, and the two sides charged toward each other. They fought almost as fiercely as if it were a real battle. When one band of horsemen retreated from the field in defeat, the other band chased after them, taking as many prisoners as they could. A captured knight was held for ransom. He had to give his horse and armor to his captor, or else pay him a large amount of money to get them back. Many errant knights made a living—and some made a fortune—by winning at tournaments.

In the fourteenth century these chaotic mock battles gave way to jousting. This was a form of mounted combat between two knights, who took their places at opposite ends of the field. Then, with lowered lances, they rode at each other as hard as they could, each trying to knock the other off his horse. These exciting contests lasted for days, because the winner of each joust then went up against other winners. At last every knight was defeated except one, the champion. He was sometimes rewarded with a prize in addition to the ransoms he had already collected.

In both tournaments and jousts, men were often killed or permanently injured. Kings and churchmen tried at various times to outlaw these violent contests. Nevertheless, they remained part of the knightly way of life throughout the Middle Ages.

# THE LANGUAGE OF LOVE

Tournaments celebrated the military aspect of the noble life, but there was also an artistic side. The noble courts of the High Middle Ages were the homes of great poetry, music, and storytelling. Much of this art celebrated romantic love. In fact, this was the first time in Europe that romantic love was considered a worthy subject for literature and song. And these odes to love were written not in Latin, the language of learning, but in the languages that people spoke every day.

The new love songs and love poems began in southern France with the troubadours, who were both poets and composers. The first known troubadour was William IX, Duke of Aquitaine. His granddaughter, Eleanor of Aquitaine, was a great supporter of troubadours and other poets. So was her daughter, Countess Marie of Champagne. Marie's grandson Thibaut, count of Champagne and king of Navarre, became one of medieval France's greatest poet-composers.

Throughout the twelfth and thirteenth centuries, troubadour songs were heard regularly in the castles of southern France. Sometimes they were performed by the poet, sometimes by another singer. Musicians playing instruments such as harp and vielle (a kind of early violin) might accompany the songs. Many of the poets and performers traveled from castle to castle. The

*A lady plays a harp to entertain herself and her companions as they relax in a castle garden. This beautiful tapestry was woven in 1420 in Flanders (now part of Belgium).*

# A TROUBADOUR SONG

One of the troubadours who was especially popular at the court of Eleanor of Aquitaine was Bernart de Ventadorn. It was said that he was the son of a peasant, but that nevertheless God gave him a noble heart, wisdom, courtesy, and the art of composing good poetry and music. Here is a selection from his song "Non es meravelha s'eu chan" ("It is no wonder if I sing"):

*It is no wonder if I sing*
*Better than any other man,*
*For my heart more to love is drawn,*
*And love's laws I excel at following.*
*Heart and body, senses and mind,*
*Strength and power—to love they are trained.*
*I am pulled toward love like a horse in rein,*
*And to nothing else can I attend.*

*When I see her, my feelings show in*
*My eyes, my face, my changing color—*
*So much do I tremble in fear,*
*As does the leaf against the wind.*
*I have no more sense than a baby,*
*For love has left me all undone,*
*And for a man so overcome,*
*A lady ought to show great mercy.*

*Good lady, I ask you for no more*
*Than that you take me as a servant.*
*For me it is reward sufficient*
*To have you as my ruling lord.*
*You see me ready at your command,*
*Heart honest, humble, gay, and courtly.*
*I trust you are not so fierce as to kill me*
*If I give myself into your hand.*

nobles who enjoyed their songs also traveled widely, and soon troubadour-style love songs spread to Spain, Italy, northern France, England, and Germany.

A common theme in these songs was a man's love for a noble lady. Often the lady did not return his love. Nevertheless, the man praised her beauty, her sense, her courtesy, and other noble qualities. He swore to be her vassal and serve her faithfully all his life. Yet he still wished that she would give him some sign of her favor. This "courtly" love was an important theme in the popular romance tales of the Middle Ages, too—and it has not gone out of fashion yet.

# 8
# CASTLE CRISES

Although castles were the homes of the most privileged people of the Middle Ages, castle life was not always easy or entirely comfortable. Fleas and lice infested all medieval dwellings, including those of the nobles. People generally bathed only once a week, if that, and clothes were not washed often, either. With mainly candles for lighting and fireplaces for heating, castles tended to be rather dim and chilly. Castle residents had little privacy.

Diseases affected the rich and powerful just as much as the poor. Nobles were able to hire physicians, midwives, surgeons, and apothecaries, but often there was little these medical people could do. The workings of the human body and the causes of disease were poorly understood in medieval Europe. So even among the nobility, death was a frequent visitor.

Discomfort and disease were bad enough, but war was worse. Castles existed because of warfare, but this was also the greatest danger to them. A lord seeking to conquer territory focused his attacks on the castles guarding it, for whoever held the castles could hold the land.

Sometimes an attacker was able to storm a castle and overrun its defenses quickly. Traitors within the walls might help the enemy

*The most feared disease of the Middle Ages was the Black Plague, which swept
through Europe in several waves. It struck in village, city, and castle alike,
and there was no cure. Queen Anne, wife of Richard II of England, died of the
plague in 1394.*

get in. More often, though, the attacker had to lay siege to the castle. With an army encamped outside the walls, the defenders were cut off from reinforcements and supplies. On the other hand, many castles had enough food stored to last a year or more. So long as the well did not dry up (as sometimes happened), the residents of such a castle were quite likely to outlast the enemy.

Attackers, however, tended not to wait passively for the defenders to surrender. A common technique was to tunnel beneath the castle walls. As soon as the tunnel was most of the way under the wall, it was allowed to collapse, and the section of wall on top collapsed with it.

If the castle was built on solid rock, so that tunneling was not an option, various siege engines, such as battering rams, catapults, and assault towers, could be used. Battering rams, used to break down walls and doors, worked best on smaller or older fortresses. Several types of catapults were employed to fling heavy stones and other missiles over the walls. Often they hurled flaming objects that set the castle buildings on fire. Assault towers were only effective if the attackers managed to fill in the castle's moat with dirt and stones. Then the tall wooden towers, full of soldiers, could be pushed right up to the walls.

If all else failed, the attackers could resort to trickery. Sometimes a small force would quietly climb the wall during the night, or get into the castle through a garderobe, garbage chute, or out-of-use well. Or the attackers might lure the castle guards out, only to chase them back in through the gatehouse. There were even times when a besieging force pretended to give up and march away. Then some of the knights would disguise themselves as merchants selling needed provisions. When they were allowed into the castle, they would seize the gatehouse and admit the rest of the army.

In spite of all these techniques, many castles survived sieges. A few were so well situated and formidable that they were never besieged at all. Numerous castles remain standing today, lasting monuments to the brave, courteous, creative lords and ladies of the Middle Ages.

*A castle under siege. The attackers are trying to tunnel under the walls. They work beneath a rolling wooden shelter that barely protects them from the rocks, torches, and other missiles hurled down by the defenders in the tower.*

# GLOSSARY

**apothecary**   a person who made medicines; a pharmacist

**bailey**   a fortified enclosure or castle courtyard

**chivalry**   the unwritten code of behavior for the ideal knight, who was expected to be brave, loyal, generous, honest, merciful, polite, respectful to women, faithful to the Church, and strong in the defense of those weaker than he

**crenellated**   (KREH-nuh-lay-ted) having battlements with alternating square or rectangular high and low sections

**curtain**   a thick, high stone wall enclosing a bailey or courtyard

**donjon** (DAHN-juhn; source of our word *dungeon*) or **keep**   a stronghold or inner tower; the strongest, inner part of a castle

**errant** (AIR-unt)   a knight without land of his own who earned his living by serving a lord for pay; *errant* means "wandering," and errant knights often went from lord to lord and from tournament to tournament, seeking their fortunes

**falconry**   a form of hunting using trained falcons, or hawks, to bring down game birds (such as ducks, pheasants, and partridges) and other small animals

**fief** (FEEF)   the land that a lord granted to his vassal; fiefs could also be other things that brought in income, such as mills, toll bridges, and markets

**garderobe** (GAHR-drobe)   an alcove with a kind of toilet seat built over a chute or drainpipe that led to a pit, ditch, or moat

**keep**   *see* donjon

**knight**   a man trained to fight as a heavily armed warrior on horseback

**manor**   an estate held by a lord, made up of his own land and land held by peasant villagers, in exchange for rents and services

**mesnie** (may-NEE)   the military men of a lord's household

**mews**   a building that housed falcons and other hawks kept for hunting

**motte** (MAHT; source of our word *moat*)   an earthen mound, usually surrounded by a ditch, on which a keep was built

**page**   a boy in the first stage of training for knighthood

**penance**   actions undertaken to show sorrow for and make up for sinful behavior

**pilgrimage**   a journey to an important religious site, such as a church that housed the remains of a saint

**portcullis** (port-KUHL-us)   a heavy gate between the gatehouse towers that could be raised and lowered

**prowess**   military skill

**saint**   a person recognized by the Church as being especially holy and able to perform miracles both during life and after death

**scutage**   money that a vassal paid to a lord instead of performing military service for him

**seneschal** (SEN-uh-shul)   a high-ranking servant who supervised a lord's household and manors; also called a steward

**squire**   a teenage boy who served and learned from a knight for two to four years in preparation for becoming a knight himself

**tournament**   a contest or mock battle between groups of knights

**vassal**   a noble who held land from a king or more powerful noble in exchange for military service and a pledge of loyalty

# FOR FURTHER READING

Child, John, et al. *The Crusades.* New York: Peter Bedrick, 1996.

Clare, John D., editor. *Knights in Armor.* San Diego, New York, and London: Harcourt Brace, 1992.

Corrain, Lucia. *Giotto and Medieval Art: The Lives and Works of the Medieval Artists.* New York: Peter Bedrick Books, 1995.

Cosman, Madeleine Pelner. *Medieval Holidays and Festivals: A Calendar of Celebrations.* New York: Charles Scribner's Sons, 1981.

Crossley-Holland, Kevin. *The World of King Arthur and His Court: People, Places, Legend, and Lore.* New York: Dutton, 1999.

Doherty, Paul C. *King Arthur.* New York and Philadelphia: Chelsea House, 1987.

Gravett, Christopher. *Castle.* New York: Knopf, 1994.

Gravett, Christopher. *The World of the Medieval Knight.* New York: Peter Bedrick, 1996.

Hart, Avery, and Paul Mantell. *Knights and Castles: 50 Hands-On Activities to Experience the Middle Ages.* Charlotte, Vermont: Williamson, 1998.

Hartman, Gertrude. *Medieval Days and Ways.* New York: Macmillan, 1952.

Hindley, Judy. *The Time Traveller Book of Knights and Castles.* London: Usborne, 1976.

Howarth, Sarah. *Medieval Places.* Brookfield, CT: Millbrook Press, 1992.

Howarth, Sarah. *What Do We Know about the Middle Ages?* New York: Peter Bedrick, 1995.

Kaplan, Zoe Coralnik. *Eleanor of Aquitaine.* New York: Chelsea House, 1987.

Langley, Andrew. *Medieval Life.* New York: Knopf, 1996.

Lewis, Naomi, translator. *Proud Knight, Fair Lady: The Twelve Lais of Marie de France.* New York: Viking Kestrel, 1989.

Macaulay, David. *Castle.* Boston: Houghton Mifflin, 1977.

Macdonald, Fiona. *First Facts about the Middle Ages.* New York: Peter Bedrick, 1997.

Nardo, Don. *Life on a Medieval Pilgrimage.* San Diego: Lucent Books, 1996.

Nardo, Don. *The Medieval Castle.* San Diego: Lucent Books, 1998.

O'Neal, Michael. *King Arthur: Opposing Viewpoints.* San Diego: Greenhaven Press, 1992.

Osborne, Mary Pope, editor. *Favorite Medieval Tales.* New York: Scholastic Press, 1998.

Platt, Richard. *Stephen Biesty's Cross-sections: Castle.* London, New York, and Stuttgart: Dorling Kindersley, 1994.

Steele, Philip. *Castles.* New York: Kingfisher, 1995.

# ON-LINE INFORMATION*

Annenberg/CPB Project. *Middle Ages: What Was It Really Like to Live in the Middle Ages?*
[http://www.learner.org/exhibits/middleages/].

Armstrong, Catherine. *William Marshal, Earl of Pembroke.*
[http://www.castlewales.com/marshal.html].

*Castles on the Web.* [http://www.castlesontheweb.com].

*Knighthood, Chivalry & Tournaments Resource Library.*
[http://www.chronique.com/intro.html].

Scheid, Troy, and Laura Toon. *The City of Women.*
[http://library.advanced.org/12834/index.html].

Stones, Alison. *Images of Medieval Art and Architecture.*
[http://info.pitt.edu/~medart].

Thomas, Jeffrey L. *Castles of Wales.*
[http://www.castlewales.com/home.html].

*Websites change from time to time. For additional on-line information, check with the media specialist at your local library.

# BIBLIOGRAPHY

Blanchard, Laura V., and Carloyn Schriber. *ORB: The Online Reference Book for Medieval Studies.* [http://orb.rhodes.edu].

Bogin, Meg. *The Women Troubadours.* New York and London: Norton, 1980.

Chaucer, Geoffrey. *The Canterbury Tales: A Selection.* Edited by Donald R. Howard. New York: New American Library, 1969.

Cosman, Madeleine Pelner. *Fabulous Feasts: Medieval Cookery and Ceremony.* New York: George Braziller, 1976.

———. *Medieval Holidays and Festivals: A Calendar of Celebrations.* New York: Charles Scribner's Sons, 1981.

Editors of Time-Life Books. *What Life Was Like in the Age of Chivalry: Medieval Europe A.D. 800–1500.* Alexandria, Va.: Time-Life Books, 1997.

Gies, Frances, and Joseph Gies. *Cathedral, Forge, and Waterwheel: Technology and Invention in the Middle Ages.* New York: HarperCollins, 1994.

———. *Life in a Medieval Castle.* New York: Harper & Row, 1974.

———. *Women in the Middle Ages.* New York: Barnes & Noble, 1978.

Hallam, Elizabeth, ed. *Chronicles of the Crusades: Nine Crusades and Two Hundred Years of Bitter Conflict for the Holy Land Brought to Life through the Words of Those Who Were Actually There.* New York: Weidenfeld and Nicolson, 1989.

Halsall, Paul, ed. *Internet Medieval Sourcebook.* [http://www.fordham.edu/halsall/sbook1.html].

Harbin, Beau A. C. *NetSERF: The Internet Connection for Medieval Resources.* [http://netserf.cua.edu/#Top].

Heer, Friedrich. *The Medieval World: Europe 1100–1350.* Translated by Janet Sondheimer. Cleveland and New York: World Publishing, 1962.

Herlihy, David. *Women, Family, and Society in Medieval Europe: Historical Essays, 1978–1991.* Providence and Oxford: Berghahn Books, 1995.

———, ed. *Medieval Culture and Society.* New York: Walker, 1968.

Hoppin, Richard H. *Medieval Music.* New York: Norton, 1978.

Irvine, Martin, and Deborah Everhart. *The Labyrinth: Resources for Medieval Studies.* [http://www.georgetown.edu/labyrinth].

Kelly, Amy. *Eleanor of Aquitaine and the Four Kings*. Cambridge, Mass., and London: Harvard University Press, 1950.

Killings, Douglas B. *Online Medieval and Classical Library*. [http://sunsite.berkeley.edu/OMACL].

Loomis, Roger Sherman, and Laura Hibbard Loomis, eds. *Medieval Romances*. New York: Modern Library, 1957.

Luria, Maxwell S., and Richard L. Hoffman, eds. *Middle English Lyrics*. New York and London: Norton, 1974.

Mertes, Kate. *The English Noble Household 1250–1600: Good Governance and Politic Rule*. Oxford and New York: Basil Blackwell, 1988.

Packard, Sidney R. *12th Century Europe: An Interpretive Essay*. Amherst: University of Massachusetts Press, 1973.

Riley-Smith, Jonathan, ed. *The Oxford Illustrated History of the Crusades*. Oxford and New York: Oxford University Press, 1995.

Schultz, Oscar. *Die Provenzalischen Dichterinnen*. Leipzig, 1888.

Shahar, Shulamith. *Childhood in the Middle Ages*. Translated by Chaya Galai. London and New York: Routledge, 1990.

———. *The Fourth Estate: A History of Women in the Middle Ages*. Translated by Chaya Galai. London and New York: Methuen, 1983.

# INDEX

Page numbers for illustrations are in boldface.